POWERBOAT INSTRUCTORS HANDBOOK

GW00702813

G19/97

Published by the
ROYAL YACHTING ASSOCIATION,
RYA House, Romsey Road, Eastleigh,
Hampshire SO50 9YA.

© 1997 Royal Yachting Association

The RYA National Powerboat Scheme was revised in January 1996. This booklet replaces the previous edition (G19/90).

Throughout this book the pronouns 'he', 'him' and 'his' have been used inclusively and are intended to apply to both men and women. It is important in sport as elsewhere that women and men should have equal status and equal opportunities.

CONTENTS

Teaching powerboating can be enjoyable, rewarding and very satisfying. It gives the experienced powerboat helmsman the opportunity to introduce others to the pleasure which he has derived from the sport.

To teach something effectively you must not only have a solid background knowledge of the subject, you must know how to pass on that knowledge to others. Even the best powerboat handler would be worthless as an instructor unless he knew how to analyse his techniques and communicate them to others.

Teaching someone to handle any high-powered vehicle is a complicated and responsible task. This handbook has been written to back up the training given on RYA Powerboat Instructor courses. It concentrates not only on the Powerboat Certificate syllabus itself, but on ways to teach each part of that syllabus.

The handbook represents a summary of teaching methods collected from many RYA recognised teaching establishments and developed over several years. It should be taken as a starting point from which your teaching techniques will develop with experience, not as a dictum to stifle further development.

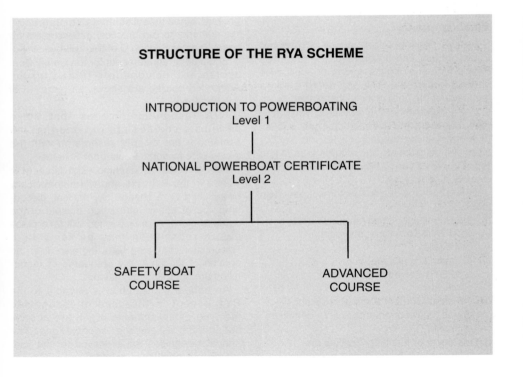

STRUCTURE OF THE RYA SCHEME

INTRODUCTION TO POWERBOATING
Level 1

NATIONAL POWERBOAT CERTIFICATE
Level 2

SAFETY BOAT
COURSE

ADVANCED
COURSE

Courses within the RYA National Powerboat Scheme are organised by RYA Recognised Teaching Establishments. These fall into three main groups:

Sailing, powerboating and diving schools or centres open to the public.

Sailing, Sub Aqua and Waterski clubs which provide tuition to their members.

Restricted organisations such as Local Education Authorities, HM Services, Lifeguards and other groups.

The Principals of RYA Recognised Teaching Establishments are the only persons authorised to issue RYA Powerboat Certificates.

Recognition of Teaching Establishments

Before recognition as a Teaching Establishment can be granted, the proposed Principal must complete a form of application obtainable from the RYA and return it with a fee to cover the cost of initial inspection.

The establishment will be visited, when fully operational, by an RYA Inspector and, subject to a satisfactory Inspector's Report, recognition will be granted. Subsequent annual and "spot" inspections are carried out at the discretion of the RYA.

During his visit, the Inspector will ascertain that:

(i) the Principal or Chief Instructor holds a valid RYA Powerboat Instructor certificate;

(ii) at least 50% of instructors hold RYA Powerboat Instructor certificates

(iii) the establishment's teaching syllabus meets the requirements of RYA certificate courses;

(iv) the onshore teaching facilities are adequate for the proposed operation;

(v) the boats to be used for instruction are suitable, seaworthy and in good repair;

(vi) all students are in possession of personal buoyancy appropriate to the type of boat in which they are receiving instruction;

(vii)the Principal properly understands the requirements of the RYA as to the proper running of an RYA teaching establishment, particularly in regard to advertising and the nature of certificate and non-certificate courses.

The RYA will then classify the teaching establishment on the basis of the Inspector's Report. Recognition for running the Safety Boat and Advanced courses will only be granted if a range of suitable boats and qualified instructors is available. This shall not prevent other establishments being granted the authority to run practical assessments for Level 2 under Section D of the syllabus.

Equipment requirements for the Safety Boat course are included in G16 and for the Advanced course are shown on page 46 of this handbook.

RYA recognition implies that some certificate courses are run and that the remainder are closely associated with the aims of the National Powerboat Scheme.

Recognition of a teaching establishment is vested in the Principal and will automatically be revoked on a change of Principal, discontinuance of active instruction or sale of the establishment. A re-inspection will take place before recognition may be reinstated. Recognition may also be withdrawn if, in the opinion of the RYA, the standards of recognition are not being maintained.

An annual subscription is payable to the RYA except in the case of recognised teaching establishments which are already subscribing as clubs or associations. The annual recognition fee is waived for the year in which recognition is granted.

Advertising and use of RYA name

Only the Principal of an RYA Recognised Teaching Establishment may use the RYA's name in any advertising material e.g. signs, brochures and advertisements. Copies of the RYA logo suitable for printing are available to Principals from the RYA Training Division.

Individual Instructors and Examiners may not use the RYA's name in any advertising or publicity material.

Administrative Procedures

On being granted recognition, each teaching establishment may open an account with the RYA for bulk purchase of publications and certificates. The latter are only supplied to the Principals of teaching establishments.

The Principal is responsible for ensuring that students' logbooks are correctly completed at the end of each course and that certificates are endorsed to show whether they have been gained on inland or coastal waters and in planing or displacement boats.

Definition

The Instructor is a competent and experienced powerboat handler who has been trained to teach powerboating up to the standard of the RYA National Powerboat Certificate, Level 2 under the supervision of the Principal of an RYA Recognised Teaching Establishment.

Note: An RYA Powerboat Instructor is not automatically qualified to teach courses run by other governing bodies.

Eligibility

Candidates should have logged at least five seasons' experience of powerboating, preferably in a range of boat types and sizes. For those who use powerboats as an integral part of their normal full-time occupation, this period is reduced to one season.

Candidates will hold the RYA National Powerboat Certificate, Level 2 and a valid First Aid certificate of a type approved by the RYA.

Instructors wishing to teach the Safety Boat course must hold that level of certificate themselves. Instructors wishing to teach the Advanced course must attend a two-day endorsement course.

Training

Candidates should apply to their Regional Coach or the RYA Training Division for a list of local Instructor courses. No candidate under the age of 16 will be accepted for Instructor training.

Candidates will attend an Instructor course run by RYA Powerboat Trainers including a moderation by an independent Trainer. The course will consist of three days including:

Principles of practical instruction
Lesson planning
Teaching styles
Use of questioning
Preparation and use of visual aids
Assessment of students' learning
Explanation and presentation of theory subjects
The structure of the National Scheme
Planning progressive teaching sessions
Preparation of boats and equipment
Teaching methods to Level 2

Assessment of the students' ability to instruct to an appropriate level with real students if possible.

Assessment

Aim

To ensure that Instructor candidates reach a required minimum standard in personal ability, background knowledge and teaching ability.

Method

During the Instructor course, candidates will be assessed afloat and ashore, being judged on:

(i) Technical ability and background knowledge
(ii) Practical instruction afloat
(iii) A shorebased training session
(iv) Planning and organisation of small group tuition.

The Examiner must be confident before recommending a pass that the candidate can teach safely and competently.

Technical ability/knowledge

This will become clear during the course, both from the practical sessions and from candidates' input to shorebased discussions. Although background knowledge may not be tested formally, it will obviously affect candidates' responses to problems posed during the course.

Practical instruction afloat

Conventionally, three methods of assessment are possible:

with beginners, if the Instructor course is run in parallel with a Powerboat course;
using other Instructor candidates as 'students';
with the Examiner playing the part of a student.

The first method is preferred by many Examiners, as it provides the most realistic assessment. If the other methods are used, the Examiner will explain the roles played by himself and/or other instructors before each session. Candidates who are in any doubt about the briefing should ask for a further explanation.

The Examiner will be looking for:
★ Good boat preparation
★ A friendly, supportive manner towards students
★ Good boat control at all times
★ Teaching progression according to the students' ability
★ Correct positioning of personnel in the boat
★ Successful demonstrations and clear explanations
★ Correct diagnosis and tactful correction of students' faults

The candidate will be judged responsible for the boat and crew the whole time, even though he may not be at the controls. Conversely, the candidate who spends too long at the controls himself, rather than reserving his driving for demonstrations, is unlikely to impress the Examiner.

When beginners are used, the Examiner will also be assessing the candidate through their reaction, looking for the three key factors which are important for successful teaching:
★ Are the students safe?
★ Are they learning anything valuable?
★ Are they enjoying themselves?

No weighting is put on any of these three, as they are inter-related. The good instructor meets each goal all the time.

Onshore Training

Candidates are not expected to be professional lecturers or polished orators. In fact, the title of this part of the assessment has been deliberately chosen to allow a practical bias. The Examiner will be looking for:
★ Overall format clear - introduction, development and summary.

★ Audible, interesting voice - right speed of presentation
★ Accurate, relevant content - sufficient material but not way beyond what the syllabus demands
★ Essential points emphasised and summarised
★ Teaching aids prepared and used as appropriate
★ Difficulties discovered and explained
★ Questions prompted and answered.

The most common faults of nervous, inexperienced candidates are to try to cram too much detail into the time available and then rush through it by speaking too quickly.

Organising group tuition

During the course each candidate will be made responsible for one or more practical sessions, as outlined above. In assessing the organisation of these, the Examiner will be looking for:
★ Clear briefings
- was the aim clearly stated/agreed?
- did the group know what was required?
- were time/area limits defined?
- was an 'abandon session' signal agreed?
★ Good group control afloat
- any unnecessary delays?
- were problems solved?
- did session achieve aim?
- did group have fun?
★ Clear debriefings
- were problems discussed?
- did instructors report progress?
★ Good group control ashore
- was it obvious who was leading?
- was whole group involved?
- was enthusiasm maintained?
★ Good relationship with others.

Overall assessment

In addition to the detailed points outlined above, the Examiner will be making a subjective assessment of each candidate as an instructor, seeing how he matches up to the qualities outlined on page 11.

These can be summarised as:

★ Enthusiasm for the sport

★ Confidence in the subject

★ Teaching ability

★ Awareness

★ Anticipation.

Candidates should be given an indication of progress during the course and in a short debrief immediately after their practical sessions, but at the end of the course the Examiner will confirm whether or not each candidate has reached the required standard as an RYA Powerboat Instructor.

The Examiner will explain in detail to unsuccessful candidates the areas in which they have shortcomings, so that these may be overcome before future reassessment.

Upon successful completion of the course, candidates will have their G20 logbooks signed by the Course Organiser, who will forward a recommendation to the RYA for issue of the Powerboat Instructor Certificate.

Coastal Endorsement

Candidates who are trained and assessed on coastal waters will have their Instructor certificates suitably endorsed. Those who are trained and assessed on inland waters will be required to attend a one-day coastal conversion course if they want to gain the Coastal Endorsement to their Instructor certificate.

Teaching of BCU, BSAC, BWSF, SAA, NABAC and RLSS Courses

For details of the requirements and methods of instructor training of the other national organisations associated with the National Powerboat Scheme, please contact the appropriate body (addresses on back cover).

The majority of your time on a Powerboat Instructor course will be spent covering detailed teaching points on the various subjects in the Powerboat Scheme syllabus, but first we need to establish the context for those teaching points.

We can do this by laying some foundations for instructional technique, which can be applied to any stage of teaching. This is intentionally a broad outline to a very complex subject and, as your teaching experience grows, so you will modify the principles given below.

Why people learn

Teaching is a form of communication; success depends on the transmitter and receiver being in tune with each other. To be an effective instructor you must know why your students want to learn.

People will start to learn if they have an incentive - a desire to learn because of the beneficial effects which that knowledge will have on them.

You might find a resistance to learning among some newcomers to powerboating, who believe it will be the same as driving a car. Your first role might be that of salesman, selling them the idea that their overall enjoyment of the sport will be enhanced by learning - in other words, you might have to provide the incentive to learning.

Why people don't learn

The most common barriers to learning are physical and mental ones, both of which must be removed by the instructor.

The most obvious physical barrier is the learning environment itself, particularly on cold, wet, windy days. People won't learn properly if they are uncomfortable or unsafe. Other physical barriers come in the form of distractions, whether from the environment, the instructor or from other students.

Mental barriers to learning range from anxiety and fear of failure to over-confidence and boredom. Many can be overcome by your confident, enthusiastic approach, stressing the interest of the course rather than any dangers. Others will be overcome if your teaching proceeds at a pace to suit the learning abilities of the students, with the flexibility to cater for differing abilities within the same group.

How people learn

People can learn for themselves by experience, by trial and error. This is usually far slower than being taught and will not always produce the required result. It does have a role in teaching, however, as lessons learnt by experience are often retained well.

People can also learn by rote - unthinking repetition of given information. One example of this is the learning of multiplication tables by young children. This may be sufficient for mechanical or "motor" skills, but does not allow for the application of judgement.

Alternatively, people can learn by reason, making deductions for themselves from established facts. In practice, good teaching is likely to combine each of these three methods of learning.

In very simple terms, practical techniques are quickly taught if the instructor follows the routine of

Demonstrate —- Practise —- Test.

Before you start that routine, though, the first step is to establish the overall framework into which the technique fits. This is an easy step to miss out if you are very experienced in the activity - and a dangerous trap for you.

Remember that what may be obvious to you may be confusing to the student; it is important to establish the context for each aspect of your teaching.

You can then give a clear explanation and/or demonstration of the technique and allow students to practise whilst you provide feedback to ensure that errors are corrected.

Finally, test to ensure that the technique and its application have been absorbed before moving on to the next stage of teaching.

In just the same way that a whole subject is broken down into topics for easy learning, complex techniques must be simplified if they are to be taught effectively. You can still use the pattern outlined above, but both the demonstration and the practice will have to be broken down into a series of simpler stages.

When this is done, it is absolutely vital that the stages are reassembled before the technique is tested and you move on to the next topic.

Safety

Under good supervision powerboating is a very safe activity, but if allowed to get out of control a powerboat can be lethal. Instructors should take great care to ensure that the exercises they set up involve minimum risk to both the participants and other water users. This is particularly important with planing craft where a collision could cause serious injury.

People can learn for themselves...

Teaching is both a skill and an art. The skills can be learnt, but the art is the product of experience and personality. An Instructor training course can provide the "motor skills" to make you a competent instructor, but only time and your own personality will allow you to develop techniques of instruction backed up by experience which will make you an excellent teacher. So what is expected of an RYA Powerboat Instructor?

Personal Skill

You must be a first class powerboat handler. You may be teaching complete novices in bad weather. You cannot teach a practical skill like powerboating if you cannot do it well yourself. If you demonstrate something, it has to work. If you're a good helmsman you will know when to intervene and when the boat can safely be left to the student's control.

There will probably be times in any lesson when a student lacks confidence in himself.

Your quiet confidence during every technique and manoeuvre, whether you are demonstrating or allowing the student to practise, will help to build the student's self-confidence. You will only have that confidence if your own boat handling skills are first class.

Communication Skills

Demonstrate, practise, test - the skilful teacher follows this simple pattern. The poor instructor assumes that because he has shown, or even worse merely told, his students how to do something then they immediately know it.

Sensitivity

We have all been on the receiving end of bad teaching at some time; one of its symptoms is "teacher insensitivity". If your students aren't learning something, it is probably your fault. The poor instructor hasn't the sensitivity to realise that there is something wrong with his own teaching.

It may be difficult to maintain that enthusiasm...

Enthusiasm

Most students arrive on a course full of excitement. That may serve as a mask for the natural fear they have about what may be involved. Your genuine enthusiasm for teaching and boating will be infectious, and will help them to overcome any nerves.

It may be difficult to maintain that enthusiasm on a cold, wet day at the end of a busy season but if you can, your students will enjoy the session whatever the weather.

Briefing

You must be able to explain what is required clearly - a difficult problem on a boat on a windy day. If you are giving a demonstration draw their attention to the part of the boat or exercise that is important at that time. For example, when demonstrating picking up a mooring, point out the wind direction and the sideways effect of the tide, etc. This will ensure that you hold their attention and they are not distracted by other craft while you are talking. As far as possible position yourself and the students so that they can see you - talking to the backs of heads is a common and basic mistake. Make your briefs exactly that - brief, the anecdotes can come later.

The Task

Students practising any skill on board must be given the opportunity to feel they are responsible for that task. Do not continually interrupt, if you have briefed well it should not be necessary. If events start going wrong, a quiet word will allow the student to correct the error. Never elbow students out of the way to demonstrate your skill - the idea is that they demonstrate theirs.

You must not, of course, allow the boat to stand into danger. The point at which you step in depends on the situation but also on the level of the student's ability. Allowing mistakes to be made is often a useful way of making a point. Always ask yourself 'Is this error a useful teaching opportunity?' not 'It'll serve him right if we pile aground'.

Debriefing

Debriefing is one of the most important skills of any instructor. Done well it is informative, positive, good natured and helpful: done badly, it can be destructive and demoralising.

At the end of the debrief students should be clear about what happened, their strengths and weaknesses and be fired with enthusiasm to try again and improve. They should never lose their self esteem or motivation.

Debrief as soon as possible after a task. If you are running an Advanced course, don't be tempted at the end of the night exercise to debrief the next morning, you will be surprised at how keen the student is to discuss the trip. Similarly, as pilotage or seamanship situations arise, debrief succinctly - underway if you can. Sometimes, particularly in rough weather, the student and perhaps you, are not up to meaningful discussions about powerboating and would prefer waiting until harbour.

You must observe each task very carefully. Often a problem develops quite a lot earlier than is perceived by the student. If necessary make notes, but do this unobtrusively as it is very threatening to sit in the boat with a notebook.

If you have time, stop the boat to debrief and take the student off the helm. A good way of debriefing is to ask the student what happened or if they would act differently next time. They will usually react by saying what was wrong, giving you the opportunity of reminding them what went right and discussing how to improve. Above all listen to what is being said to you. Many instructors used to taking command and issuing instructions neglect the student's comments and are therefore unaware as to whether anything is getting across or not.

The aim of this section is to give course organisers an outline of the points to consider when planning a powerboat course. Every course has four elements - the students, the instructors, the fleet/teaching facilities and the syllabus. It is the task of the course organiser to ensure that they all fit together harmoniously.

Course planning is simply a matter of starting with a list of factors related to each of these four elements, and sorting them into an order.

Within the majority of RYA recognised teaching establishments, powerboat courses are run at the same time as other training activities. Given the maximum teaching ratio of 1:3 for levels 1 and 2, it follows that student numbers will probably be governed by the number of suitable boats available and instructors will be nominated according to student numbers.

Safety boat and advanced courses can be conducted with a ratio of 1:6.

That provides the first cornerstone of planning: the overall size of the course itself. After that, things will start to slot together to take account of the following:

Students

Overall costing, hence fees charged
Advertising of course
Booking form and health declaration
Confirmation of insurance cover
Preparation of joining instructions etc
Dealing with special needs
Catering/accommodation
Logbooks, certificates, handbooks etc

Instructors

Abilities of existing staff
Need for specialist input
Pre-course instructor briefing
Feedback from instructors during course
Final assessment

Fleet/teaching facilities

Suitability of fleet and operating areas
Personal buoyancy for all students and instructors
Engine/boat maintenance and service schedules
Additional equipment: marks, MOB dummies, radios etc
Onshore teaching area and seating
Visual aids

Syllabus

Overall length of course
Formal introduction/conclusion to course
Timings of each session, including debriefings
Launch and recovery timings
Refreshment breaks
Balance between theory and practice
Daylight and/or tidal considerations

There is no great mystique to lesson planning, merely some logic. Ignore the basic rules, however, and your students will be struggling to understand where a particular technique or piece of background fits into the overall scheme of his learning.

Every lesson should be structured so that it has a beginning, a middle and an end. If that seems like an obvious statement, rest assured that it is included in this handbook after years of experience in assessing potential instructors.

The beginning or introduction must include the title, aim and relevance of the lesson, so that students will understand how and why what they are about to be taught fits into the wider framework of the scheme.

It should also include an outline of the method to be used, so that students will know whether they are merely expected to sit and listen, join in a discussion or whether they are expected to take part in a practical activity.

It could include the limitations on what is going to be taught, if relevant. An example of this could be the introduction to the owner maintenance lesson of a Level 2 course, when the instructor explains that he does not intend to teach students how to become professional outboard mechanics!

The middle of any lesson contains the bulk of what is to be taught. Its content should be arranged in a logical order and built in stages, with confirmation of learning at the end of each stage.

If you have difficulty deciding just how much to put into any lesson, try breaking it down into the headings of:

What must be covered

What should be covered

What could be covered

and then rehearse to see how it fits into the time available. You can then edit the lesson by cutting out or shortening some of the less important detail.

The end or conclusion of a lesson must contain a summary of the main points. It should also contain a link to the next lesson and could include references to further material from which students could learn more.

In order to make the task of the Powerboat Instructor a little easier, detailed lesson planning for Levels 1 and 2 courses is given later in this handbook.

"Didactic vs experiential" is how it's summarised in the syllabus for the Instructor training course, but what exactly does that mean in practice?

Didactic literally means "meant to instruct", or "having the manner of a teacher". In other words, a didactic style implies the precise packaging and transmission of information from instructor to student, so that the latter can achieve the aim of the lesson.

Few would argue that it is an efficient way of teaching practical techniques but it does have a number of disadvantages as a method of teaching theoretical subjects.

The first is that it represents very passive learning for the students, who are simply recipients of information. Attention spans are therefore likely to be short.

The second is that information is inevitably restricted to that which the instructor has planned. If he has misjudged the existing knowledge of the students, and is repeating information which is already known, then the session is wasted.

The third is that it encourages instructors to stick to a familiar format and even to a certain set of teaching notes and visual aids. If someone is teaching the same subject repeatedly in the same way, it will inevitably lead to staleness of approach.

What are the alternatives?

At the opposite end of the teaching spectrum is controlled learning, where the instructor's task is simply to provide the right environment and the right materials for students to learn for themselves.

It represents very passive learning...

The strongest argument for this approach is that students will accept and retain best that knowledge which they have learnt from their own involvement or experience.

The principal disadvantage of this style is the time it takes, quite apart from the fact that it could lead students to question the "value for money" of their course!

It is also surprisingly difficult to get the learning environment and resource materials exactly right, so that students will arrive at the desired conclusion at the end of the learning period.

As you might expect, the happy medium comes somewhere between these extremes, and each instructor's teaching style will evolve with experience. Certain topics lend themselves to the traditional style of instruction - almost a "doing it by numbers" routine, whilst others are crying out for a different approach. Let's look at a couple of examples.

Task-centred teaching

Traditionally, lectures on tides have started with the words:

"Tides are caused by the gravitational pull of the moon and, to a lesser extent, the sun. When sun and moon are in line..."

It's all accurate stuff, but deadly boring to many students and guaranteed to lose their attention after a few minutes. An alternative approach could be for the instructor to sketch out an imaginary coastal trip of a few hours' duration, and then ask the students to say how and where the tide will affect a powerboat.

The answers could include launching, getting out of an estuary, speed and comfort of any passage, seastate, conditions around a headland and the time and difficulty of recovering the boat onto its trailer.

Those topics could then form the basis of the lesson, along the lines of "What do you need to know about tides for successful launching and recovery?" and so on.

The benefit - student involvement throughout the session because they have posed the problems which are solved as a group activity. The drawback - none except that the instructor must have a good grip of the syllabus to ensure that nothing is omitted. The instructor must also have enough knowledge beyond the limit of the course syllabus to ensure that he can deal with any unexpected questions.

Brainstorming...

For the second example, let's look at the subject of Safety Equipment in Level 2. Here's a classic way to send students to sleep: all you need to do is reel off a long list of equipment and where it should be stowed. You may have covered the syllabus, but can you really be proud of your teaching?

One alternative which guarantees student involvement is brainstorming, followed by a problem solving session. For those who haven't tried it, the brainstorming process can best be explained as a means of getting all the group's thoughts, however nonsensical or impractical, down on paper.

This can be done either as one large group, or possibly more effectively, as a number of small groups. Given the subject, each person in the group simply calls out every word or idea which comes into his head and it is recorded. In this case, the instruction would simply be to say every-thing which comes into your head when the words "safety equipment" are mentioned.

If the group is small, the responses can be written on a piece of paper; for larger groups a blackboard or flip chart is needed. When inspiration dries up, the group leader has the task of sorting the words into groups or themes for the ensuing session.

...and Problem Solving

Once the instructor has extracted the raw material from the class, the second stage of the lesson can begin. For this, the students can be divided into small groups and each one given a specific task or problem associated with the subject. For example, one group might be given the task of working out a "shopping list" within a budget, for a powerboat owner intending to operate within a defined area.

Another group might be given the "ideal" shopping list and asked to prepare a stowage and maintenance plan for all the equipment. A third group might be given the "ideal" shopping list and asked to prepare notes for a crew briefing on how to use the equipment.

If the time allowed for each of these projects is chosen carefully, the group's enthusiasm will ensure that the whole subject is covered in very little more time than the instructor's monologue would have taken.

These are just a couple of examples of how teaching styles could be varied to suit either the syllabus or a particular group of students. The good instructor will sit down at the end of each course and ask himself: "Did the students get as much out of that course as they might have done? If not, how could I improve it next time?"

Equally, if an experiment in teaching style does not work first time, the instructor has a responsibility to his students to ensure that any resultant gaps in their techniques or knowledge are filled before the course ends.

Teaching adults...

There is much common ground between the teaching of adults and the teaching of children. When dealing with adults, however, there are a few special points to bear in mind.

1. Adults tend to have a greater fear of failure than children. They are therefore more reluctant to appear foolish in front of a class. You should concentrate on rewarding ideas and not on making those who give wrong answers feel inadequate.

2. Adults for whom "being lectured" is their only experience of being taught may be reluctant at first to become involved in discussions or other teaching techniques. They expect the instructor to talk continuously and dislike having to contribute themselves.

You will have to push against this initial dislike; once the students have overcome it they will learn more quickly and enjoy themselves more. Don't give anyone the opportunity to opt out. To encourage others, congratulate those who do join in initially.

3. Adults are much more vulnerable to sarcasm than children, who tend to be used to it.

4. The greater part of adult learning since leaving school will have been by "problem-solving" and personal experience. Use this to your advantage and let "problem-solving" from information you supply be one of your teaching methods, but remember that this approach usually takes longer than instruction.

5. An adult's academic interest in the subject is not always compatible with his practical ability; the gap sometimes widens with age.

Don't give anyone the opportunity to opt out

...and children

Although generalisations are difficult, young people usually make better students than adults, learning faster and with better retention. The very fact that children are used to classroom teaching can, however, make life difficult for you. If their motivation is not high, it will be lowered further by a dull lecture in the classroom.

In addition, children learning within a group of relative strangers may initially be very shy about contributing answers. This in turn makes it difficult for the instructor to assess how much is being absorbed, without resorting to testing which again makes the process seem like school. Once you have overcome the shyness, however, you could find the opposite problem of having to control class input to the level which allows you to teach.

The lecture is potentially the worst possible way of teaching a practical subject like power-boating. It has been described as a race between the lecturer and the audience to see who can finish first.

Remember the saying:

I hear and I forget,

I see and I remember,

I do and I understand.

The mere statement of a fact is no guarantee that listeners have received that fact as you understand it, or will necessarily remember it for any length of time. It is far better to teach a practical subject in a practical way whenever possible. There are theory elements of the syllabus, however, which can only be taught ashore. Bear the following points in mind when teaching:

★ **Consider the room layout.** Anything you say or do will be pointless unless your students can see and hear you. Remember that you are in charge; move furniture if necessary. Encourage students to fill lecture rooms from the front. Make sure your room is comfortable, cool and well ventilated.

★ **Keep lectures short.** Twenty minutes is about the right length of time to maintain students' attention without testing or a break. Don't over-run.

★ **Outline your aims** at the beginning of a lecture and summarise the essential points to remember at the close. A handout stating the important facts is useful, but should not be given out until the end of the lecture. Handouts distributed at the beginning will only be read by students when they should be listening to you.

★ **Give your lecture a structure:** Introduction, Development, Summary, Test.

★ **Link salient points to dramatic examples.**

★ **Consider the age and experience of your audience.** (See notes on teaching adults.)

★ **Choice of language.** Avoid complicated terms but define any which are essential.

★ **Choose your position.** Where and how you stand will have an effect on your lecture. Standing behind a desk or lectern may appear more formal but puts a barrier between you and your audience. Sitting on a table at the front of the class may be too relaxed for some talks. Watch polished speakers and assess their use of body language. Don't hide behind your visual aids (see below).

★ **Involve your audience.** Speak to your audience - all of them. Don't talk to the ceiling, the floor or the wall at the back of the classroom. Try to make eye contact with every member of the audience at some stage. As alternatives to a monologue, use question and answer techniques, discussions, games etc. Learn and use students' names.

★ **Avoid irritating mannerisms.** Your Instructor course will help to identify habits of which you may have no knowledge.

★ **Avoid distractions.** Like mannerisms, any distractions which take your students' attention away from what you are saying will damage your lecture. If you are giving a lecture outside because of good weather, arrange the group such that they are facing away from any distractions and so the sun is in your eyes, not theirs.

★ **Practise writing on blackboards.** Prepared Overhead Projector acetates are preferable to copious boardwriting with your back to your students. Never talk to your blackboard, always to your students. If you are not using or have finished with a blackboard, rub it clean to avoid distraction.

★ **Don't bluff.** If you don't know the answer to a question - say so. Your students would far rather have an honest "I don't know, but I'll find out," than a bluffed answer. Having said that, you should always ensure that you have a wider knowledge of your subject than the basic facts contained in your lecture.

Where and how you stand will have effect...

★ **Don't be afraid to test.** Ten questions, which are immediately marked by the students themselves, will help to reinforce your teaching.

★ **Avoid sarcasm, humiliation or rudeness.** Try not to let any of your prejudices alienate members of the class. In particular, avoid patronising students of a very different age group from your own and avoid sexism.

★ **Don't try to be funny unless you are naturally witty.** The Instructor course will help to appraise you of your natural level of humour.

★ **Avoid the lecture entirely** if the subject is better taught another way. At some centres, for example, there is no "ropework" lecture or session as such. Knots are introduced only when needed for a particular purpose. In that way each knot and the reason for tying it are always linked in a practical environment.

★ **Finally, remember** that your lecture will have succeeded only if all your students leave it having learnt the main facts which you needed to communicate and eager to learn more.

The aim of this short section is to highlight the value of questions, both to and from your students. The enormous benefit of using questions in teaching is that they require two-way communication; the instructor can tell whether the students are involved and whether the information he is transmitting is being received.

Questions to students

Questions to students can be used to fulfil three purposes - to teach, test or trigger more learning.

Teaching by question and answer is a technique which relies on the instructor being able to pose the right questions at the right time in order to elicit the required response.

Used well, it will enable students to maintain their attention spans far longer than in a lecture, simply because of their involvement. There is an added motivation for attention, because they do not know who is to be questioned next.

Clearly there are difficulties in using this technique when introducing a technical subject to a group of novices, but these can be overcome with the right choice of questions.

For example, imagine that you are giving a talk about hull shapes to a Level 2 group. One way of doing it would be to show 35mm slides of an example of each generic type and rattle off the characteristics as outlined on page 36.

How much more effective would your teaching be if you showed simple plan and elevation diagrams of each type and posed the questions:

"Why do you think thedory is more stable at rest than the Deep V hull?" or

"What will happen to the inflatable in a strong crosswind?"

Questioning to test is most effective if you follow the pattern of Pose - Pause - Pounce. Pose the question to the group then pause to allow students time to think of the answer.

During this time your gaze will rove around the group until you pounce on someone for an answer.

If you identify one of the group before asking the question, the others will lose attention, knowing that they are not going to be asked.

If a student doesn't know the answer, don't chastise him for it but move on to someone who does. If none of the group know the answer to something which has been covered, you clearly did not explain it properly - thus questions serve to confirm that your teaching has been effective.

Questions can also be used to trigger more thought, possibly linking what has been covered to a future session to ensure continued interest, or encouraging students to learn more outside the framework of your teaching.

This is particularly important in the National Powerboat Scheme, because of the nature of the courses. The good instructor is one who has encouraged his students to want to learn much more about the sport and improve their boat handling with more practice.

Questions themselves fall into two categories - closed (or direct) which require a simple answer and open (or indirect) which lead on to more thought. In general, closed questions are used for simple testing whilst open questions are more effective for teaching and triggering further thought.

Questions from students

Similarly, questions from the group can be considered under different headings: relevant or irrelevant, taught or not yet taught.

Relevant questions covering material which has already been taught can be tackled in two ways. You can either explain the material again or, better still, throw the question back at the group. If it is answered, the questioner is satisfied and you know that your teaching has been at least partially successful.

If nobody can answer, it confirms that you haven't taught the point effectively. Try again, preferably in a slightly different way.

Relevant questions covering material which has not been taught may be answered briefly (if there is time and the answer will not confuse or distract the group).

Alternatively, delay the question by explaining that it will be covered later, asking the student to remind you if the answer does not become clear.

Irrelevant questions serve as a distraction to the group and must be disposed of as quickly as possible. A student who persists in asking such questions is probably doing so to draw attention to himself.

A quiet word away from the group to explain the effect he is having should be enough. If not, you will have to dispose of the questions firmly, but not rudely, in front of the group. You will have their sympathy.

Finally. if asked a question to which you do not know the answer, there is only one course of action. Admit that you don't know, and tell the questioner that you will find the answer as soon as possible. Then do it.

Whatever you do, don't bluff. If students realise that you're bluffing, it will destroy their confidence in you as an instructor.

PREPARATION AND USE OF VISUAL AIDS

Analysis of sources of information to the brain shows that sight plays a proportionately greater part in the learning process than all the other senses. Sight accounts for about 75% of input, hearing about 15% and the other senses share the remaining 10%. A picture may not be worth exactly 1000 words but this analysis shows why the use of visual aids is so important - and why the avoidance of visual distractions is necessary.

Visual aids are usually used either to help explain difficult concepts or to build up complicated ideas or techniques. They may also be used to emphasise or reinforce certain key points in your teaching.

Basic Principles

★ Relevance - Visual aids should not be produced for their own sake. They must be relevant or they become a distraction.

★ Clarity - Diagrams must be easily understood and not contain irrelevant detail. They must be readable by the furthest of your audience. Any visual aid which cannot be seen by everyone is neither visual nor an aid.

★ Timing - Don't produce visual aids until they are needed; they will only distract your audience if displayed too soon. Dispose of them after use.

★ Display - Try to display a visual aid in a dramatic manner. Students will remember something for longer if it is linked to a highlight.

★ Involvement - A display of neatly tied knots on a board is much less effective than students attempting to tie the knots themselves, although the knotboard will be useful reference after the lesson.

Use the other senses. An aid which does something and which can be passed around is more valuable than something which is merely displayed. Beware of moving on to another topic while your visual aid is still circulating. Nobody will listen to you if they have a

toy with which to play. Equally, use the mechanism of some visual aids to 'punctuate' your lecture and put in 'paragraphs' e.g. switching off the OHP between acetates, lights on/off between slides.

★ Yourself - Don't forget that you are a walking visual aid with optional sound yourself. Think about your mannerisms, delivery, position etc and their effect on the class. Never hide behind another visual aid so that your audience cannot see you properly. Finally, dress for the occasion. Although boating is a practical sport, don't let your appearance serve as a distraction to your audience. A good general rule is to dress as well as the best dressed of your audience - that way, nobody will be offended.

Nobody will listen to you if they have a toy...

Types of visual aid

It is often said that the best visual aid available to the instructor is the boat itself, but the more advanced your teaching, the less true that statement becomes. Each of the other visual aids in common use has certain advantages and drawbacks.

Blackboard or penboard

Once the mainstay of classroom teaching, the blackboard or chalkboard has the advantages that it is readily available, does not require power, can be used continuously and can be seen by large numbers.

The disadvantages are that although adequate for simple messages or drawings it is unsatisfactory for detailed work to be done when the audience is present. The information cannot be stored and successful use depends on a practised style.

The more recent alternative of the penboard has the advantage of being less messy to use but all the other drawbacks of the blackboard, the most important one being that it is impossible to talk to your audience effectively while writing on the board.

Flipchart

Popular for business conferences, the flipchart has many of the characteristics of the blackboard but the twin advantages that it is portable and information can be prepared in advance, stored and used repeatedly.

Overhead Projector

Properly used, the OHP is undoubtedly the most versatile visual aid employed in teaching centres. Although it requires power, it can be used in daylight and without the instructor losing eye contact with the audience.

Although it is possible to write or draw as you speak, most instructors prefer to prepare OHP acetates in advance. You can enhance them by the use of colour and by using overlays to build up or break down complex concepts or techniques.

Once a few operating tricks are learnt, the OHP is simple to use effectively but you must avoid the temptation to put too many words on an acetate. Remember that words are not visuals, even though they may be used to trigger thoughts or retain ideas.

35mm transparencies

Most effectively used to bring the boat into the classroom, a set of 35mm transparencies can be produced at virtually every club or centre and tailored to the exact needs of the instructor.

Commonly used for subjects like hull type, engine installations, buoyage and some boat handling techniques, "home-made" transparencies have the added advantage that the boats and background will be familiar to the students.

Apart from requiring careful preparation and scripting in the first instance, 35mm transparencies have the disadvantage of requiring both power and a darkened room. Against this, they can lend accuracy and realism to your teaching. Be ruthless in editing your transparencies into a final teaching sequence. If one is not really needed, throw it out.

Video

Apart from the entertainment value of non-marine material on residential courses, there are two ways of using video when teaching.

The first is to show previously prepared material, whether professionally made or filmed locally. The majority of professional training videos are intended to be used in parts, rather than right through in one showing.

This allows you to use the highly effective technique of interactive teaching - select the topic you want to teach and intersperse video teaching with practice afloat until the technique is mastered. Careful planning is essential, including a clear introduction of what is being covered on the video extract and a rehearsal to cue the tape to the right place.

The second approach is to use a video camera afloat with your group. This enables the instructor to record examples of good and bad techniques and manoeuvres so that

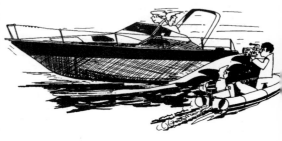

Get as close to the action ... as you can

students learn by seeing their own mistakes.

The number of instructors who can use video afloat is extremely limited. Three useful rules until you gain more experience are:

1. Forget about the attractions of the zoom lens. Get as close to the action with as short a focal length as you can. The resulting picture will be far steadier and hence less likely to induce seasickness in the audience later;

2. Turn off the microphone. Even the professionals separate the roles of cameraman and commentator. Your "off-the-cuff" comments are likely to offend and be less helpful than a later commentary over a silent video;

3. Choose definite techniques or manoeuvres to film and switch off in between. Nothing is more aggravating for your students than having to sit through two hours of playback for the two minutes of their own appearance.

Models

Ranging from simple shapes used for collision avoidance talks to detailed models of powerboats, the scope for models is limited only by the ability of the builder.

In general, a model should have only enough detail as is required to ensure a full understanding of its role. Over-complication may be satisfying to the creator but must not detract from its use as a visual aid.

Over-complication ... must not detract from its use...

Group Control

When working as a Powerboat Instructor, much of your time will be spent teaching two or three students in a single boat. Regardless of who is actually sitting at the controls, you are in charge of the boat and directly responsible for the safety and actions of the students. You should therefore sit within easy reach of the steering and throttle controls. The time will come, however, when as an experienced instructor you will be in charge of a group of students and instructors. Your control of that group has a direct effect on their learning and their enjoyment, as well as their safety.

Successful group control afloat depends on careful planning and anticipation. Time afloat will be time wasted unless each session has a clear aim and each instructor knows how much he is expected to achieve. Those messages must be made clear in each briefing.

Group control problems aren't restricted to the water. Before you end any onshore teaching session or briefing, ask yourself whether the students:

a) know exactly what they are going to do next and

b) if going afloat, know where and when they are to meet back ashore for the debriefing.

To make sure the whole session runs smoothly, remember that launching and recovery times might need to be coordinated to avoid slipway congestion. The limits of the operating area should be clearly defined and instructors should be made aware of each other's tasks to avoid conflict and confusion.

Once the session is under way, you should be continually asking yourself "What is the worst thing that could happen now?" and then "What are the others going to do while I'm sorting it out?" In this way, you should be able to anticipate disasters and prevent them happening.

Communication afloat

The worst possible way of passing information is to shout it from one moving powerboat to another, yet it is surprising how often this technique is used.

Try to establish a policy of never saying anything above the sound of your engine. When you want to talk to students in your boat, simply slow down and stop.

If you need to talk to the crew of another boat, first get them to stop. The motorists' hand signal meaning "Slow Down" is almost universally understood. If you use it, you can then come close along-side and talk in a normal voice, while both engines are in neutral or stopped completely.

If you're planning a long conversation like this, do monitor your combined drift to ensure that you won't hit each other (if hull types are unsuitable/unfendered) and that you won't drift into anything else!

If you need to brief a whole group of powerboats afloat, you have failed...failed to brief properly ashore or failed to run an effective session. You now have two choices; either brief each boat individually or get the whole group ashore and brief properly.

To get them ashore, you simply have to institute your "Abandon session" signal. That has to be visual, rather than aural, and capable of being seen over the entire operating area for as long as is necessary.

Finally, if you are running a large powerboat course in an exposed location, where the excitement of rough weather handling might cause instructors to forget your briefing on the operating area, consider the use of hand-held VHF radios.

There are all sorts of practical problems, including stowage, waterproofing and simply hearing what is said over the background of engine noise, but with planning these can be overcome to a certain extent.

At the majority of centres, however, the use

of such sets is limited to urgent radio traffic between a boat and the base station ashore, rather than from boat to boat.

Boats used for RYA powerboat training must be sound, suitable for the area of operation and carry the following equipment:

- Paddles or oars
- Bucket or bailer
- Bridle secured to towing eyes
- Towline
- Spare starting cord and minimal tool kit
- Survival bag or thermal protective aid
- First aid kit containing large wound dressing and triangular bandages in a watertight container
- Bower anchor sufficient for safety boat and any towed craft
- Chain and warp as appropriate to the area
- Distress flares - 2 orange smoke and 2 pinpoint red, or day/night flares

The notes which follow are based on the maximum teaching ratio of 1:3. Large powerboat courses will simply consist of many teaching groups made up in the same ratio; such groups may of course be combined for some of the briefings and talks.

These talks should be kept as brief as possible, as the course is essentially a practical one with the emphasis on work afloat.

The syllabus of the Level 1 course has been designed to suit the needs of all newcomers to powerboating, whether their interest lies in planing or displacement boats. It is expected that the majority of demand will be for the former, but to make this section comprehensive, teaching points are given for both outboard and inboard engines and both displacement and planing boats.

Each Level 1 certificate should be endorsed to confirm whether the training has been given in a planing or displacement boat, whilst details of the course and boat type should be entered in the personal log section of the student's G20 logbook.

1. Launch and Recovery

Aim
To teach students to launch a boat from a trailer or trolley using a ramp or slipway.

Method
Briefing session, 10 minutes, to outline procedures, assess launching site and point out hazards. This could usefully be run in conjunction with that for Item 2, in which case the time should not exceed 15 minutes.

This will be followed by practical experience associated with launching and recovery before and after each practical session in the remainder of the course.

Teaching Points
Although you will want to get the students afloat as quickly as possible, do not waste the opportunity of instilling the basic principles of good launching and recovery techniques.

The practical sessions during a Level 1 course are likely to be run using only one boat. If a student has bought/is planning to buy a boat of another hull type, you could outline any major differences in launching/recovery technique.

Initial assessment
  Suitability of area
  Sea conditions
  State of tide
  Ownership of slipway/ramp
  Slipway width, angle and surface
  Extension of slipway underwater

Launch
  Use of jockey wheel/handbrake
  Boat floated off, not pushed
  Deployment of crew
  Trailer/ trolley parking

Recovery
  Reassessment of conditions
  Will slipway take car?
  Care in use of trailer winch

RYA *1875·2000*
125 YEARS

MEMBERSHIP

Isn't it time you joined?

FOR THE FUTURE OF BOATING

Isn't

As one of the estimated 7 million people in Britain who are involved in recreational boating, your right to enjoy your own pleasure in your own way is under ever-increasing threat of restriction - from Government, from Europe's rule-makers, from pressure groups with other interests.

The RYA is the national organisation which exists to promote the interest of everyone who goes on the water for pleasure.

The more personal members it has, the louder its voice is heard when it comes to defending your interests.

Its voice becomes your voice.

it time you joined?

Benefits of Membership include

- Access to expert advice on all aspects of boating from legal wrangles to training matters

- Special members' discounts on a range of products and services including boat insurance, books, videos and class certificates

- Free issue of certificates of competence, increasingly asked for by everyone from overseas governments to holiday companies, insurance underwriters to boat hirers

- Access to the wide range of RYA publications, including the quarterly magazine

- Third Party insurance for windsurfing members

Special Offers for RYA Members

- Free Internet Access with RYA-Online

- Up to 33% off subscriptions to IPC Yachting Magazines

- A Healthcare Cash Plan

- A privilege price structure for purchasing a Volvo car

- Save £££'s with e-commerce deals secured for the RYA through the Buying Team

www.rya.org.uk

Membership application form

If you have previously been a member and know your membership number please enter here

When completed, please send this form to:-
Royal Yachting Association, RYA House, Romsey Road, Eastleigh, Hampshire, SO50 9YA

Please use Block Capitals

Type of Membership Required: (tick as applicable)

☐ **Personal £25** (*£23* if you pay by Direct Debit)

☐ **Family £40** (*£38* if you pay by Direct Debit)

☐ **Under 21 £10**

Please indicate your main boating interest by ticking one box only

W	SC	SR	PR	MC	PW
☐	☐	☐	☐	☐	☐

W=Windsurfing   SC=Sail Cruising
SR=Sail Racing   PR=Powerboat Racing
MC=Motor Cruising   PW=Personal Watercraft

	Title	Forename	Surname	Date of Birth	Male	Female
1.						
2.						
3.						
4.						

Address

Town ___ County ___ Postcode ___

Home Phone No. ___ Day Phone No. ___

Facsimile No. ___ Mobile No. ___

Email Address ___

Signature ___ Date ___

Instructions to your Bank or Building Society to pay by Direct Debit

DIRECT Debit

Please fill in the form and send to:
Royal Yachting Association, RYA House, Romsey Road, Eastleigh, Hampshire, SO50 9YA. Tel: 023 8062 7400

Name and full postal address of your Bank/Building Society

To The Manager	Bank/Building Society
Address	
	Postcode

Name(s) of Account Holder(s)

Bank/Building Society account number

Branch Sort Code

Originator's Identification Number

9	5	5	2	1	3

Reference Number

Instruction to your Bank or Building Society
Please pay Royal Yachting Association Direct Debits from the account detailed in this instruction subject to the safeguards assured by The Direct Debit Guarantee. I understand that this instruction may remain with the Royal Yachting Association and, if so, details will be passed electronically to my Bank/Building Society.

Signature(s)

Date

Banks and Building Societies may not accept Direct Debit Instructions for some types of account

---

OR YOU CAN PAY BY CHEQUE

Source Code **077**	Centre Stamp	Cheque enclosed	£	Made payable to the 'Royal Yachting Association'	**Office use only:** Membership No. Allocated

Correct positioning of boat on trailer
Effects of stream and windage
Use of rope or solid bar between trailer and car

2. Preparation of Boat

Aim
To make students aware of the need for certain equipment and the need for pre-launch engine and boat checks.

Method
Briefing session, probably combined with Item 1.

Discussion ashore, based around boat, outlining engine/fuel preparation and need for certain equipment.

Teaching Points
Outboard engines
> Security of clamps or bolts
> Engine tilted
> Controls connected (if appropriate)
> Safety lanyard (kill-cord)
> Fuel tanks filled, secured and vented
> Fuel lines connected and primed
> Reserve fuel
> Battery state and security

Inboards and Outdrives
> Controls working
> Fuel tanks filled
> Outdrive tilted
> Reserve fuel (if appropriate)
> Battery state and security

Equipment
> Alternative means of propulsion
> Personal buoyancy carried/worn
> Painter shorter than boat
> Anchor/warp stowed
> Bucket/bailer stowed
> Warps/fenders ready for use
> Engine spares/tools stowed
> Emergency equipment stowed
> Coastal equipment as appropriate

3. Boat Handling

Aim
To teach engine procedures and basic handling in a single boat, together with the importance of keeping a good lookout at all times.

This session also provides the opportunity to instill the idea of consideration for other water users, particularly those in less manoeuvrable craft, swimmers, divers and canoeists.

Method
Short briefing outlining aims, followed by practical instruction afloat. Instruction should be given as a series of tasks, each one being first introduced and demonstrated by the instructor.

Teaching Points
Engine starting (Outboards)
> Gear shift in neutral
> Fuel line primed
> Use of choke/cold start
> Appropriate throttle setting
> Use of starter cord or ignition key
> Return choke/cold start
> Check for water cooling telltale

Engine starting (Inboards and Outdrives)
> Pump bilges
> Operate extractor fans
> Switch on fuel
> Use of choke/cold start/preheat
> Then as for outboards

Engine stopping
> Gear shift in neutral
> Stop engine by key/switch/button
> Importance of running carburettor dry if leaving engine for some time
> Fuel switched off/line disconnected
> Engine tilted (outboard/outdrive)

Engine controls
> Use of tiller or remote controls
> Importance of sitting opposite tiller on tiller-steered engines
> Importance of smooth but firm movement of gear shift
> Potential damage through misuse

Loading
> Fore and aft trim; balance
> Manufacturer's guidelines on maximum numbers
> Effect on stability and performance

Awareness of others
Importance of lookout
Effect of wash at all speeds
Consideration for others, especially
swimmers, canoeists, divers & dinghies
Pollution: fuel and oil spillage

IRPCS
Steering and Sailing Rules (5-10, 13-19)
Speed limits; Bye Laws

Planing boats
Use of kill-cord
Low speed manoeuvres: steering, effect of
wind/current/tide
Manoeuvring astern; risk of swamping
High speed handling:
    initiating planing; throttle control
    slowing down; risk of pooping

Displacement boats
Handling ahead: steering, pivot point
Slowing down
Amount of way carried in neutral
Changing gear; need to pause in neutral
Handling astern:
    propwash, steering difficulty,
    load on rudder

4. Leaving and Coming Alongside

Aim
To teach the basic principles of these manoeuvres, so that students will be able to practise the techniques safely.

Method
A short talk (max 10 minutes) to establish principles, followed by a demonstration by the instructor and supervised practice by each student.

This session could end with the reminder that the approach to a person in the water follows the same principles as picking up a mooring in non-tidal water.

Teaching Points
Leaving berth
Preparation; engine running
Communication with crew
Bow or stern first?
Effect of wind, current or tide
Consideration for other craft
Stowage of warps and fenders.

Coming alongside
Preparation of warps/fenders in open water
Approach; use of wind, current or tide
Escape route if manoeuvre is abandoned
Communication with crew
Securing boat; use of cleats
Allowance for changes in wind or tide

Picking up a mooring
Preparation of rope/painter
Direction and speed of approach
Securing line

5. Being Towed

Aim
To prepare students for engine failure and instill basic principle of salvage.

Method
A short talk (max 10 minutes), preferably followed by a practical session. If possible, the group of three students should be split so that one accompanies the instructor in the towing boat and the others remain in the towed boat. In successive sessions the roles can be changed, as long as the instructor stays in the towing boat.

Teaching Points
Principles
Importance of agreeing terms first
Towed boat should offer own line

Procedure
Securing tow line; strong points
Trim of boat; engine tilted

This course is probably the most important part of the Scheme, forming the basis of boat handling techniques which are needed for the specific tasks implied in the Safety Boat and Advanced courses.

Although some students will have completed a Level 1 course, the Level 2 syllabus assumes no previous knowledge; some of the topics detailed below repeat parts of Level 1.

SECTION A: PRACTICAL

1. Launch and Recovery

Aim
To teach students how to launch and recover their boats from road trailers or launching trolleys, and provide background knowledge to prepare them for a variety of launching sites.

Method
Briefing session, 15 minutes, to outline preparation of boat, assessment of launching site, procedures for launching and existence of local hazards.

Practical experience associated with launching and recovery before and after each practical session in the remainder of the course, ideally with a variety of craft.

Teaching points
Initial assessment
Sea conditions
State of tide
Ownership of slipway/ramp
Slipway width, angle and surface
Extension of slipway underwater

Preparation
Lightboard; prop bag; trailer ties
Warps; fenders
Engine secured/tilted; fuel

Launch
Use of jockey wheel/handbrake
Consideration of wheel bearings

Use of rope or solid bar between trailer and car
Boat floated off, not pushed
Deployment of crew
Heavy gear loaded after launch
Trailer parking

Recovery
Reassessment of conditions
Will slipway take car?
Care in use of trailer winch
Advantages of break-back trailers
Use of trailer guide bars
Correct positioning of boat on trailer
Effects of stream and windage
Use of rope or solid bar between trailer and car
Care of wheel bearings
Security of trailer ties
Fitting of prop bag and lightboard

2. Boat Handling Under Way

Aim
To teach precise boat handling at low speeds, principles of high speed handling as appropriate, awareness of Collision Regulations and consideration for other water users.

Method
The subject can conveniently be split into the topics listed below. Each can then be tackled separately, in most cases by means of a briefing to outline the principles involved, followed by a practical session.

The length of these sessions will be sufficient to ensure that every student has the opportunity to practise each new technique until the instructor is confident that the principles have been properly understood.

Fast manoeuvres should initially be carried out in comparatively calm conditions, until the instructor is confident of the students' abilities.

It is suggested that a slightly different approach is adopted for the teaching of awareness of others and the application of the International Regulations for Preventing Collisions at Sea.

This could first be covered as an illustrated talk, using whatever visual aids or models are available. The principles thus taught can then be reinforced in every practical session, by question and answer technique whenever other craft or water users are encountered.

Teaching Points
Awareness of others
Importance of lookout
Effect of wash at all speeds
Consideration for others, especially swimmers, canoeists, divers and dinghies
Pollution: fuel and oil spillage

IRPCS
Steering and Sailing Rules (5-10, 13-19)
Lights and Sound Signals (22,23,34)
Speed limits
Local Bye Laws

Loading
Fore and aft trim
Balance
Safety: manufacturer's guidelines
Effect on performance and consumption

Propeller angle/immersion
Anti-cavitation plate (outboards)
Engine trim: manual or remote

Planing boats
Use of kill-cord
Low speed manoeuvres:
> steering, effect of wind/current/tide

Manoeuvring astern; risk of swamping
> slowing down; risk of pooping

Turning in confined area:
> 360 degree turn
> alternate use of ahead and astern power
> wheel on full lock before gear engaged

Holding off jetty/moored boat
High speed handling:
> crew safety and comfort
> initiating planing; throttle control
> slowing down; risk of pooping

High speed manoeuvres:
> warning to crew
> need to hold throttle throughout
> S and U turns
> effect of cavitation

Displacement boats
Effect of stream or current at all times
Handling ahead:
> steering, pivot point

Slowing down
Amount of way carried in neutral
Effect of windage on topsides
Changing gear; need to pause in neutral
Direction of propeller rotation
Handling astern:
> propwash, steering difficulty, load on rudder

Turning in confined area:
> alternate ahead/astern power
> full helm on favoured side throughout

3. Securing to a Buoy

Aim
To teach students how to approach and secure to a mooring buoy safely and to leave that mooring under control.

Method
A short talk (five minutes) outlining the principles should be followed by a practical demonstration. Each student should then be given the opportunity to practise.

Only after the correct approach has been taught and understood, and only if conditions allow, the instructor may then choose to demonstrate the wrong approach (downwind/downtide) to highlight the problems.

Teaching Points
Preparation
Mooring line ready
Boathook, if appropriate
Communication with crew
Crew disposition

Approach
Check how other boats are lying
Approach into wind or tide
Slow, controlled approach
Plan escape route

Making fast
    Length of mooring line
    Secure to mooring, not pick-up buoy
    Attached to mooring or looped back aboard
    Use of fairlead
    Protection against chafe

Departure
    Prepare return line
    Ensure engine running well
    Check all lines clear of propeller

4. Anchoring

Aim

To advise students on choice and stowage of anchor and warp, and to introduce the principles of anchoring a powerboat.

Method

A short talk (max 15 minutes) could effectively be given on the beach, where the principles of how the anchor "digs in" and how it is "broken out" can be demonstrated, rather than merely talking about them. This talk can be developed, if well planned, to illustrate the effectiveness of different types of anchor and the need for a short length of chain to reduce chafe.

The talk should be followed by a practical demonstration and supervised practice.

Teaching Points
Equipment
    Types of anchor in common use
    Weight related to boat size
    Security of anchor when underway
    Short length of chain: chafe
    Length/size of warp
    Stowage: reel/coil/basket/bucket
    Bitter end of warp secured

Preparation
    Choice of anchorage
    Estimate/check depth
    Estimate swinging room required
    Coil/flake enough warp to reach bottom
    Remainder ready to unreel/uncoil
    Remove anchor from stowage

Approach
    As for mooring
    Boat stopped before anchor let go

Making fast
    Confirm anchor is holding
    Pay out enough warp (4-5 times depth)
    Use of transits
    Warp through fairlead: chafe

Departure
    Engine running first
    Use of power to take weight off warp

5. Coming Alongside

Aim

To teach the principles of berthing alongside and leaving a jetty, pier or other boat, so that students will be able to practise the techniques safely.

Method

A short talk (max 10 minutes) to establish principles, followed by a demonstration by the instructor and supervised practice by each student.

Once the correct approach has been taught and fully understood, the instructor may demonstrate the wrong approach (downwind/downtide) to highlight the problems. It should be pointed out that this technique is included in the Level 2 test because it is sometimes needed in an emergency or in a very confined area.

Teaching Points
Leaving berth
    Preparation; engine running
    Communication with crew
    Bow or stern first?
    Effect of wind, current or tide
    Springing out of confined space
    Consideration for other craft
    Stowage of warps and fenders

Turning in berth
    Use of warps and fenders

Coming alongside
    Preparation of warps/fenders in open water
    Approach; use of wind, current or tide
    Escape route if manoeuvre is abandoned
    Communication with crew
    Final approach; engine control
    Securing boat; use of cleats
    Allowance for changes in wind or tide
    Length of mooring lines in tidal harbours

Assessment: is it safe?
Choice of side to come alongside
Use of warps and springs
Possibility of damage caused by rolling

6. Man Overboard

Aim

To teach students how to return to a given spot in the water and stop. Although clearly important for recovery of a person in the water, the technique also marks an important stage in basic boat handling.

Method

The subject can conveniently be divided into three sections:

how to get back to the MOB, how to get him aboard, aftercare.

The first of these will be covered in a practical way, with a short briefing followed by demonstration and practice. The other sections should be covered by discussion or question and answer.

Care should be taken to make the exercise as realistic as possible, using nothing smaller than a 25 litre (5 gallon) plastic drum almost full of water as the MOB dummy. Students should not be expected to enter the water at any stage.

When demonstrating, supervising practice and assessing the technique, instructors should ensure that the dummy is dropped overboard immediately alongside the boat, to simulate a real incident. This reinforces the need for an immediate turn to keep the propeller away from the MOB.

Teaching Points
Prevention
Crew never allowed to sit on foredeck
Crew encouraged to sit, rather than stand
Helmsman to give warnings before starting from rest and before sudden manoeuvres
Importance of kill cord for helmsman
Action
Alert crew; observe MOB
Immediate turn to keep prop clear
Method of turn and approach:

U turn/circle
Direction of final approach
Out of gear as boat closes MOB
Throw line or reach for MOB
Engine cut completely
Recovery
Self help
Boarding ladder; rope strop
Help by helmsman/crew
Aftercare
Advice to MOB
Don't panic
Watch boat; raise one arm
Inflate lifejacket; use whistle

7. Disabled Craft

Aim

To prepare students for potential problems afloat, including grounding, hull damage and engine failure.

Method

A short talk outlining the principles, followed by a practical session.

The more realism which can be injected into this session, the greater will be its effect. Individual instructors and Principals, however, will know the limits to which practical sessions can be taken without damage to equipment and injury to personnel.

If possible without injury and damage, students should be given the opportunity of dealing at least with engine failure in open water and refloating after grounding. With experience, Principals could develop this session to cover a variety of realistic problems.

Teaching Points
Boat adrift
Drifting towards safety or danger?
Use of anchor if depth permits
Alternative propulsion - effectiveness
Controlling drift/ paddling towards moorings
Assessing cause/ rectifying engine failure
Self help before seeking help
How to seek help

Boat damage
Alter heel/ trim to bring damage above waterline
Plug leaks temporarily and head ashore
Bailing under way

Grounding
Prevention; awareness of surroundings
Reversing off; engine partially tilted
Changing trim; lightening boat
Use of paddles; get out and push!
Check for damage to hull and engine
If stranded; lay out anchor and wait for tide

Towing
Speed/ angle of approach
Passing and securing towline; use of bridle
Signals/ communication
Speed of tow
Manoeuvring in confined areas
Casting off tow

Being towed
Offer own line; agree terms
Secure towline; agree signals
Tilt engine and trim boat bow up

SECTION B: ONSHORE TEACHING

1. Types of Craft

Aim
To introduce and compare the characteristics of the hull types in general use, so that students are better able to make a choice between them.

Method
Depending on group size, this session could either be run as an illustrated lecture or as a walk around a boatpark or foreshore.

Teaching Points
Basic difference between displacement and planing hulls.
Characteristics of:

Displacement craft
Easily driven
Maximum hull speed governed by length
Good directional stability
Performance not greatly affected by load
Seakindly motion in bad weather
Often of rugged construction

Inflatables
Portable
High stability
Very high buoyancy
High load carrying capacity
Wind affected
Low directional stability
Rough, wet ride at speed
Soft contact with other boats etc
Relatively short lived

Rigid-hulled inflatables
Combines advantages of V-hull with inflatable
Good directional stability
High buoyancy
Exceptional seaworthiness in bad weather
High load carrying capacity
Soft contact with other boats etc
Requires trailer or trolley
Some makes are relatively short-lived

Dories and cathedral hulls
Good directional stability at low speeds
Good load carrying capacity
High stability, even at rest

Buoyancy usually built in (between skins)
Uncomfortable at high speed in waves
Requires trailer or trolley

V shaped hulls

Low initial stability at rest
Good directional stability at speed
Buoyancy must be built in
Deep V gives soft ride at speed
Shallow V gives harder ride
Requires trailer or trolley

2. Engines and Drives

Aim

To introduce the different engine configurations and compare their advantages. To teach students the importance of safety checks, owner maintenance and regular professional servicing.

Method

The subject is best covered by teaching in small groups, preferably in a workshop. It is an area where the instructor sometimes hands over to his staff mechanic or bosun, or possibly to a representative from a local engine dealer.

Teaching Points

Characteristics of:

Outboards

Easily accessible
Choice of short/standard/long shaft
Adjustable trim
Can be tilted for beaching
Can be removed for storage/service
Usually separate, portable tanks
Usually petrol; two stroke or four stroke
Engine acts as rudder
Very poor steering in neutral

Inboards

Permanent installation
Shaft usually exposed below hull
Serviced in situ
Permanently installed tanks
Usually diesel
Drives propeller via shaft; separate rudder(s)

Outdrives

Essentially a combination of characteristics
Usually reserved for high power units
Engine inboard, usually at stern
Petrol or diesel; permanent tanks
Outdrive leg with advantages of outboard

Fuels

Risk of petrol compared to diesel
Two stroke - mixed in tank or oil injection
Unleaded petrol - refer to handbook
Tanks - portable vs permanent; security
Fuel lines - kink free; clear of working areas

Batteries

Stowage; security; maintenance; wiring

Maintenance

After use:
run engine dry to empty fuel in carb
fresh water wash-down
Regular checks by owner
Changing plugs
Changing propeller (outboard only)
Emptying water trap on fuel filter
Oil and grease schedules
Controls and linkages
ImportancRegular servicing by dealer/agent

3. Ancillary and Safety Equipment

Aim

To introduce students to the use and stowage of important equipment.

Method

The subject is probably best covered in small groups around a boat on a trailer ashore, giving students "hands on" experience of the equipment.

It is an area where "task-centred" learning might be more effective than more formal teaching. For example, students might be given the tasks of listing the equipment carried, its stowage, and reading the operating instructions for flares, fire extinguishers etc. In addition, centres could provide spent flares so that students can practise using the firing mechanisms.

Teaching Points

Alternative propulsion
Spare engine
Paddles/oars
Jury rig (sail) from clothing etc

Emergency equipment
Torch
Flares; types, stowage and use
Fire extinguisher; stowage and use
First Aid kit
Spare buoyancy aid or lifejacket.

SECTION C: COASTAL

This is an inherent part of all Level 2 courses run on coastal waters. It may also be used as the basis of a separate one-day conversion course for holders of inland Level 2 certificates who wish to extend their knowledge and practical ability.

1. Practical Application of Section A

The teaching points below apply specifically to coastal waters and should be taken in conjunction with those given above under Section A.

Apart from the influence of the tide, the most significant difference between inland and coastal courses is the potential for teaching rough water handling at sea.

The infrequency of suitable conditions, particularly in the summer months, will result in many students leaving a Level 2 course without first hand experience of rough water powerboating.

In such circumstances, the instructor should ensure that enough information is given to allow the candidate to tackle rough water, knowing what to expect and knowing what action to take.

Teaching Points

Launch and Recovery
Need to obtain accurate local weather forecast
Sources of forecasts; need for awareness of weather changes
Characteristics of lee and weather shores
Difficulties of launching from beach:
wave height; bumping on trailer/trolley; danger to crew
Use of anchor to haul off
Harbour regulations and signals
Informing others of plans and number of crew
Planning for return:
state of tide; expected weather conditions

Boat Handling under Way
Effect of tide on all slow speed manoeuvres
Changes in sea state: wind with/against tide
Pilotage, importance of buoyed channels etc

Rough water handling

Characteristics of high speed craft:
jumping from wave to wave
effect of landing on chine
comfort/safety of crew
effect of prop leaving water
risk of hull damage
reduced visibility
unreliability of most compasses
risk of burying bow downwind

Characteristics of displacement craft:
motion into, not over, waves
reduced speed and visibility
rolling in beam seas

Choosing best course and speed:
advantage of oblique course upwind
avoid swamping downwind

Securing to a Buoy

Effect of tide continues when boat is
secured: boat can be sheared when
moored by use of rudder/outboard
Boat will be affected by tide immediately
mooring is released
Danger of swimming from moored boat in
tideway

Anchoring

As above for mooring
Anticipation of depth changes as tide
rises/falls

Coming Alongside

Approach is almost always into tide
Use of tide when leaving berth

Man Overboard

Both MOB and boat are affected by tide
Danger of both being swept into other
craft/obstructions

Disabled Craft

Use of sea anchor at bow to prevent
swamping
Need for flares; principles of use
Role of RNLI and HM Coastguard

2. Chart and Compass

Aim

To introduce students to the information
contained in charts and the use of chart and
compass in powerboats. By the end of this
session, students should know enough to be
able to identify features and relate them to a
chart, and vice versa.

They should also be able to identify shallow
areas, shipping lanes and obstructions from
the chart and relate their position afloat to
these areas.

Method

This section is not intended as a navigation
course, and instructors should be careful not
to exceed the aim stated above. Students
seeking a greater depth of knowledge should
be recommended to take an RYA Day Skipper
shorebased course.

Teaching in small groups around a chart will
be more effective than a lecture to a large
group.

Teaching Points

Charts

Name; number; scale
Measuring distance from Latitude scale
Use of compass rose
Laying off headings/bearings
Depths: colours/contours/figures
Concept of chart datum
Important symbols: use of 5011
Buoyage: cardinal and lateral
Tidal diamonds/ tidal stream diagrams

Compass

Usual notation
Outline concept of variation
Siting of steering compass
Causes of deviation
Use of handbearing compass in
small boats
Action in reduced visibility

3. Tides and Tidal Streams

Aim

To introduce students to sources of tidal
information and to teach a general awareness
of the effects of tides and tidal streams.

Method

A group session to introduce the concept of tides, their effect on the powerboater and sources of information could usefully be followed by some short shorebased exercises in small groups. These would enable students to gain first hand experience of using tide tables and charts for basic passage planning.

It is easy to make the subject unattractive to many students; please note the comments on teaching styles on pages 15 - 17. Please also beware of going into too much detail and remember the aim of the session.

Teaching Points

Sources of information
Tide tables and almanacs
Tidal stream atlases
Charts - tidal diamonds

Definitions
High and low water
Springs, neaps
Chart datum (LAT)
Range, rise
Ebb, flood
Effect of wind with/against tide on sea state

Height prediction
Rule of Twelfths or Admiralty method

Observation afloat
Flow around fixed objects
Boats on moorings (not always accurate)
Buoys leaning downtide

Relative strengths
Narrow channels
Deep vs shallow water
Third and fourth hours of ebb/flood
Off headlands

As outlined in the Powerboat Logbook G20, any candidate with the necessary experience may gain the Level 2 Certificate by direct assessment, rather than at the end of a course.

The most common reasons for doing this are when the Certificate is needed as the basis of an International Certificate of Competence or when an experienced powerboat handler wishes to gain the higher awards in the National Powerboat Scheme.

The test may be undertaken at any RYA recognised Powerboat Teaching Establishment, using either a boat provided by the establishment or the candidate's own boat, subject to its approval by the Examiner as suitable.

Assessment will follow the format of the practical test shown below, and will be carried out by the Principal or an RYA Powerboat

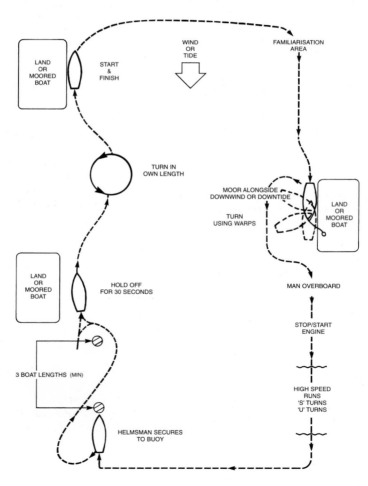

Instructor nominated by him. In addition, candidates will be required to answer a theory paper to test their background knowledge.

Before the test, the assessor should remind the candidate that the manoeuvre of coming alongside downwind/downtide is regarded as unseamanlike, but is tested because it may be necessary in an emergency.

Criteria for assessment

The notes below provide the standard for assessing driving ability during the test. They have been phrased as positive points - the assessor should simply be able to tick them all off on an assessment sheet.

If a candidate fails to show any of the points marked *, the assessor may not award a pass on that section of the test. Further attempts may be made. If a candidate fails to show any of the other points listed, his attention should be drawn to them in the debrief.

Coming alongside downwind/downtide
Did candidate:
Communicate effectively with crew?
Show awareness of other water users?*
Prepare warps/fenders or check crew had done so?*
Choose correct angle of approach?*
Control speed of approach?*
Stop boat in required place?*
Maintain control of boat while warps were secured?*

Turning using warps
Did candidate:
Communicate effectively with crew?
Position fenders effectively?
Prevent contact between boat and jetty/pontoon etc?*
Secure boat adequately?*

Man overboard
Did candidate:
Execute immediate turn to keep prop away from MOB?
Observe MOB or instruct crew to do so?*
Demonstrate correct direction and speed of approach?*
Make suitable contact with MOB?*
Stop engine before attempting retrieval?*

Stop/start engine
Did candidate:
Choose suitable area?*
Shift into neutral before stopping engine?
Check gear/throttle/choke before starting?*
Start engine successfully?*
Check engine water cooling after starting?*
Warn crew before moving off?*

High speed manoeuvres (if appropriate)
Did candidate:
Use kill-cord?*
Choose suitable area?*
Show awareness of other water users?*
Warn crew before each manoeuvre?*
Initiate planing effectively?
Trim boat properly?
Look around before S and U turns?*
Control speed on U turns?*
Deal with cavitation on turns?

Securing to buoy
Did candidate:
Communicate effectively with crew?
Prepare warp?
Choose correct angle of approach?*
Control speed of approach?*
Secure boat effectively?*
Depart from mooring safely?*

Manoeuvring astern
Did candidate:
Steer boat effectively in reverse?*
Control speed to avoid flooding over transom?*
Complete exercise?*

Holding off
Did candidate:
Start parallel to and approx 1m off jetty/pontoon?
Maintain position to within 1/2 boatlength?*
Use gears calmly?
Pause during gearshifts?*
Avoid damage to engine or gears?*

Turning in own length

Did candidate:

    Demonstrate understanding of principles?*

    Pause during gearshifts?*

    Apply steering lock before engaging gear?

    Complete exercise?*

Coming alongside

Did candidate:

    Communicate effectively with crew?

    Show awareness of other water users?*

    Prepare warps/fenders or check crew had done so?*

    Choose correct angle of approach?*

    Control speed of approach?*

    Stop boat in required place?*

    Maintain control of boat while warps were secured?*

    Check security of warps?

TEACHING THE
SAFETY BOAT COURSE

The aim of this course is to introduce the techniques used in powerboats escorting racing fleets of dinghies, windsurfers and canoes, providing safety and rescue cover for training fleets and assisting in race management. It is strongly recommended that a member of the rescue crew should hold a first aid certificate (or should have experience of first aid).

As participants must hold the National Powerboat Certificate Level 2, it is likely that the course organiser will have to arrange for some or all to take the short Direct Assessment for the certificate before the Safety Boat course starts.

The emphasis throughout the course is on practical work, so that participants can experience and solve real problems, rather than simply discuss them. Practical sessions should be structured following the pattern of 'Demonstrate - Practise - Test' outlined on page 9, with the instructor posing real problems to the group involving the recovery of dinghies and windsurfers. Opportunity should be given for every participant to supervise each type of rescue outlined in the syllabus.

Ropework should be introduced as needed, rather than all being covered in one lecture. For example, the rolling hitch could be introduced in the briefing prior to a towing session, while heaving line use could be practised prior to the recovery of a dinghy on a lee shore.

Boats should be equipped appropriately for their operating area, using the list in the G16 Safety Boat Handbook as a guide. Dinghies and windsurfers must be available for practising rescue techniques.

Teaching Points for Kayak or Canoe Rescue (supplied by the British Canoe Union)

The main purpose of an escort boat for a fleet of kayaks or canoes is to back up the instructor, and particularly to allow for unexpected illness or other unforeseeable situations arising. Normally the instructor is expected to undertake rescues and return students to their craft and the escort boat coxswain should always check whether his or her services are required, except in an obvious emergency. A system of communication between the coxswain and the canoeing instructor should be established at the outset.

The main thing to remember when rescuing a swamped kayak is that if one end of the boat is pulled out of the water and emptied, leaving the other end flooded, the kayak is likely to break in half if the rescuer then levers down in order to raise and empty the flooded end. It is essential to achieve a gradual emptying by keeping the kayak horizontal on its side and exerting a steady pull on the cockpit rim until most of the water has been evacuated. It can then be lifted upside down onto the gunwhale of the escort boat and see-sawed until empty.

Canoes (open canoes) should be turned upside down and merely lifted from the water by one end and pulled across the escort craft .

The intention of the Advanced Course is to provide training and assessment for the serious amateur and the professional user.

It is essential to the credibility of the scheme that the course is delivered to a constant national standard by competent instructors. Instructors should qualify by attending an Advanced Instructor training course run by a Powerboat Trainer.

Pre-course Experience

Advanced students will need to be good boat handlers before enrolling. Candidates must hold the Powerboat level 2 certificate and should have extensive experience of powerboat handling. There is not time to teach chartwork and navigation on the course so please ensure that students have navigational knowledge. A Day Skipper shorebased course completion certificate is acceptable. If they do not hold this, they need to convince you that they have an equivalent level of knowledge.

Venue and Equipment

The course must be taught at a coastal venue. Large estuary locations are ideal as they provide all weather training with a variety of navigational features.

A sea going planing boat, usually a RIB, must be provided with the following equipment:
Compass
Lights conforming with IRPCS
VHF radio (may be portable)
Anchor and cable
Tow line
Torch
Basic tool kit and spares
Heaving line
Paddles
Flares - 2 hand held red, 2 orange smoke

The school should also provide:
Laminated or waterproof charts
A GPS set (may be hand held)
Tide tables
Pilotage notes
Plotting instrument

Each crew member should wear a 150 Newton lifejacket with a DoT (UK) approved lifejacket light.

Passage Making

The course should include a pilotage exercise. It is helpful to plan a day trip which can be undertaken again at night. A circuit around lit buoys and/or entry into a lit harbour is ideal. NB. on Powerboat Trainer courses candidates are sometimes asked to find unlit marks at night This is beyond the level of the Advanced course.

Pilotage

Pilotage is best done by eye rather than electronic navaids. The exercise is not a race and it can be valuable to stop at intervals to emphasise any important teaching points.

This is primarily a teaching session rather than an assessment but you should ensure that each student has had a genuine opportunity to plan and implement at least part of a passage (and not just follow the boat in front).

Emphasise that from a known position it should be possible to use a chart and compass to identify the next mark or other significant features. (From an unknown position it is very difficult.)

Night Passage

A working knowledge of light characters is essential. Given the potential hazards of sending planing boats into the dark, it is worth having an instructor or 'minder' who knows the area on each boat. If this cannot be arranged, a very careful brief and assessment of the student's ability is necessary. Divide the trip so that each student has a chance to pilot the boat.

Radio communication is essential.

Ensure that everyone in the boat keeps a lookout, particularly in areas where high speed ferries operate. Remember that as the Instructor, you are responsible for the safety of all the boats.

Meteorology

Make the meteorology as practical as possible. You need sufficient information to make decisions about whether and where you can operate your boat. A full shipping forecast is often less relevant than a more detailed local forecast. Powerboat passages are rarely more than a few hours and your consideration of weather should reflect this. The hardest decision is whether to set out. Give students help on how you make this decision.

Syllabus Notes

Preparation for sea

By the end of the course the students should understand or have a knowledge of basic engine checks and how to remedy defects which do not require workshop support, ie plugs, fuel, etc. Ensure that the equipment is secured for coastal passages.

Boat handling

Hull forms and their handling characteristics
Deep and shallow V formations
Dead rise or flare
Cathedral hulls
RIBs

Rough Weather

Significance of tidal stream on sea conditions
Steering and power control through waves
Correct use of trim tabs or power trim in rough weather
Strategy up and downwind

Boat Handling in a Tidal Stream

Turning in confined spaces, awareness of the effect of the tidal stream
Steering to transits across a tidal stream
Effect of tidal stream on alongside berths

- choose a fairly tight berth in a marina or equivalent
Mooring to buoys. - choose buoys in tidal streams - awareness of eddies etc
Advanced students should have good awareness of ground speed and should be able to hold the boat on station into a tidal stream.

Passage Making

The course must include the planning and undertaking of a passage in sight of land and visual marks
The pre-plan should be quite detailed and include a consideration of tidal heights and streams
Identification of charted features, particularly hazards such as shoals and rocks

Chartwork

Depths and drying heights
Buoyage IALA and lateral
Light characters Fl, Iso, F, Oc
Bearings and distances
Tidal heights - basic knowledge at standard ports
Tidal Streams - use of atlas or diamonds - interpolation by eye (ie springs, neaps or midway)

GPS

Its uses - waypoint navigation
World-wide availability
Its limitations - less useful for very accurate pilotage. Dependant on battery etc
The techniques of high speed navigation, using the pre-plan to determine courses, times and distances to next mark

Pilotage

Students should be able to enter and depart from a well charted port
Importance of avoiding shipping channels where possible
Observing speed limits and awareness of harbour hazards and traffic signals
Awareness of clearing lines and transits to avoid hazards
Use of soundings to avoid shoals and determine a position line

Meteorology

Knowledge of where to obtain weather information eg. local radio, telephone, fax etc.

Using weather and tidal information to predict likely sea conditions and make passage planning decisions.

Rules of the Road

IRPCS, in particular rules:- 5, 7, 8, 9, 13-17 and 23.

Students should be able to identify power and sailing vessels by night. Identification of types of ship by night is not required except a knowledge of the lights of tugs and trawlers. Fatalities have occurred by powerboats avoiding tugs by steering around their sterns.

In general a powerboat should not get into a position where a large vessel is required to give way.

Use of Engines

Sufficient knowledge to make checks and rectify defects which do not require workshop support on both petrol and diesel engines

On petrol engines concentrate on electrical and fuel system.

On diesel engines, bleeding fuel, filters and water systems, changing transmission belts.

Changing propeller and shear pin.

Emergency Situations
(covered as theory)

Fire prevention - dangers of petrol and use of extinguishers
Sector search
Helicopter rescue

VHF Radio Distress Call

A distress call is sent when there is GRAVE AND IMMINENT DANGER to a vessel or person and IMMEDIATE ASSISTANCE is required

---

Switch on power, switch on radio, select *CH16*, turn to high power. Push press-to-transmit switch and speak slowly and distinctly.

- MAYDAY, MAYDAY, MAYDAY

- This is (Boat's name 3 times)

- MAYDAY (Boat's name)

- Position (see below)

- Nature of distress

- Any extra information which might help

- Over

- Take your finger off the transmit button

MAYDAY is the international distress signal 'I require immediate assistance' and include number of people on board, whether you are going to abandon ship or have fired flares etc 'Over' means please reply

An Urgency Call

An urgency call is used when you have a VERY IMPORTANT MESSAGE to send covering SAFETY.

The advantage of an urgency call is that it lets the world know that you are in some sort of trouble without launching all the rescue services at that moment.

- PAN PAN, PAN PAN, PAN PAN
  All stations (3 times)
  This is (Boat's name 3 times)

- Position

- Nature of urgency

- Assistance required

- Over

Prefix a call to a British coastal radio station with PAN PAN MEDICO to get medical advice.

Keep transmitting at regular intervals even if you don't get a reply so the rescuers can home in on you.

EPIRB Emergency Position Indicating Radio Beacons will raise the alarm and help the rescue services to find you.

Positions must be given in Lat and Long or TRUE bearing FROM a charted position with distance off (e.g. Position 235° from South Head, 5 miles).

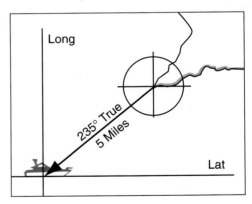

If it's a DECCA position, say so as any errors can be duplicated in the rescue craft's set.

Lifeboat Rescue

Lifeboats can home in on your VHF radio. They may ask you to give a long transmission by counting slowly.

If you can see the lifeboat but think they may not have identified you or there are other small boats in the area, use a pin point red flare. Give them your position by radio relative to them if possible, ie 'we're 20° to the right of you, 1/2 mile'...etc.

Once the lifeboat arrives, do what you are told. Remember they are there to save lives, not salvage boats.

At night if you need to show your position with a searchlight, shine it straight up for a lifeboat and straight ahead for a helicopter.

Helicopter Rescue

Once a helicopter is in your vicinity you must not, of course, use parachute flares.

Brief your crew early. It will be too noisy later. The pilot will fly over to assess the situation then stand off to brief you over the radio. He will probably ask you to head into wind but in a small boat with a casualty on board you may be asked to simply stop.

The aircraft will approach with you on its starboard side so that the pilot and winchman can see you. They will use one of two methods to reach you, either:

While the helicopter is hovering at about 50 feet the winchman will be lowered directly on to the boat. He will have an earthing wire attached to the line. Allow this to touch the sea before making contact.

or

A weighted line (hi line) will be lowered.

Gather this in and use it to control the winchman as he is lowered to you. Never tie it on. Take care to stow the line so that it can be run out easily. Once on board the winchman will take charge. If he decides to lift you off with a helicopter strop, remember to keep your arms by your side. The helicopter crew will ensure that you arrive at the helicopter with your back to the door. Serious casualties will be lifted off by stretcher.

Remember to thank the crew afterwards.

Search Patterns

Sector Search

Mark the datum with a lifering, dan buoy or similar, if a lifejacket is used it should have a coil of line tied to it to act as a sea anchor. It

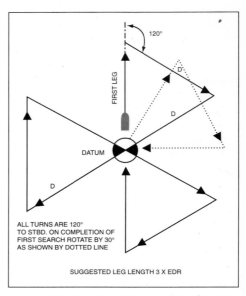

ALL TURNS ARE 120°
TO STBD. ON COMPLETION OF
FIRST SEARCH ROTATE BY 30°
AS SHOWN BY DOTTED LINE

SUGGESTED LEG LENGTH 3 X EDR

is essential that the datum marker is free to drift in any tide or current; a close by navigation mark or similar anchored marker should not be used. The initial heading of the vessel should be North, 000°. As the vessel proceeds North away from the datum marker a steady count should be made out loud, whilst glancing at the marker occasionally. When the stage is reached where the marker is visible for approximately 50% of the time, that indicates the expected detection range (EDR). The leg length is suggested to be three times EDR (this gives a maximum area search with a good quality of search).

At the end of each leg turn 120° to starboard and proceed for the same distance, as shown in the diagram.

Example:

On leaving the marker heading North and counting, the marker appears to be visible for 50% of the time as the count reaches 47, this can be rounded to 50, the leg length would then be a count of 150.

After completing the first leg the vessel is turned 120° to starboard and a further count of 150 started. The vessel then turns 120° to starboard again and the count restarted. When the count reaches around 100 (two-thirds of the way down the leg) the marker should become visible straight ahead. Once the marker is sighted it can be steered for, thus correcting any errors made.

The pattern is then continued to completion of the first circuit. If the suggestion of heading North on the first leg is utilised, then the headings are all easily worked and remembered, being 000°, 120° and 240°.

If by this stage the search is unsuccessful the pattern can be reorientated 30° to starboard and repeated. Again assuming 000° for the first leg of the first search, the new headings become 030°, 150°, 270°.

If the sector search has been completed, ie two full circuits and there is a requirement to continue searching, then an expanding box search should be started.

Expanding Box Search

Conventionally, the leg length on an expanding box search is 75% of the expected detection range. Assuming the expanded box search is following the sector search, expected detection range has been established visually. As this is effectively the third search of the area it is considered acceptable (and far less complicated for a shocked crew)

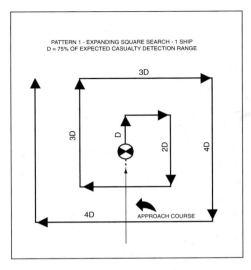

PATTERN 1 - EXPANDING SQUARE SEARCH - 1 SHIP
D = 75% OF EXPECTED CASUALTY DETECTION RANGE

3D

3D

D

2D

4D

4D

APPROACH COURSE

to use 100% of EDR if preferred. From the example given previously, legs one and two would be a count of 50, legs three and four a count of 100, legs five and six a count of 150 etc. Again for ease of completion it is suggested that the headings are North, South, East and West.

RYA POWERBOAT INSTRUCTOR

Training Course Completed

Venue _____ Date _____

Course Organiser
RYA Powerboat Trainer (name in caps)_____

Signature _____

Assessment Completed

Venue _____ Date _____

Approved by
RYA Powerboat Trainer (name in caps) _____

Signature _____

ADVANCED POWERBOAT INSTRUCTOR

Assessment Completed

Venue _____ Date _____

The candidate has demonstrated competence as an
Advanced Powerboat Instructor to the standards laid down by the RYA

Approved by _____
RYA Powerboat Trainer (name in caps)

Signature _____

POWERBOAT TRAINER

Recommendation

I confirm that the candidate has the experience and technical competence
to be trained as a Powerboat Trainer within the RYA National Powerboat Scheme.

Regional Coach (name in caps) _____

Signature _____

Training Course

I confirm that the candidate has successfully completed the course
and has demonstrated competence in all areas required.

Signature _____
National Coach

NATIONAL POWERBOAT SCHEME
INSTRUCTOR LOG

DATE	TYPE OF BOAT	HOURS INSTRUCTING	LEVEL OF COURSE	MAX WIND SPEED	AUTHORISATION Establishment/Principal
TOTAL C/F					

		TOTAL B/F			
DATE	**TYPE OF BOAT**	**HOURS INSTRUCTING**	**LEVEL OF COURSE**	**MAX WIND SPEED**	**AUTHORISATION** Establishment/Principal
	TOTAL C/F				

The list which follows does not include books on powerboating. Those recommended as background reading for students are listed in the G20 logbook.

The books outlined below cover many aspects of training - in sport, industry and professional work. Many techniques are common to different disciplines; you simply have to decide how best to apply the authors' ideas to your needs.

Coaches Guide to Sport Psychology

Rainer Martens
ISBN 0-87322-022-6   Human Kinetics
A detailed subject presented in a down-to-earth style to remove the mystique.

Inshore Navigation

Tom Cunliffe
ISBN 0-906754-31-3   Fernhurst Books
A clear explanation of all the basic pilotage and navigation needed by the Powerboat Instructor, to give you a greater depth of knowledge needed to teach the Level 2 and Advanced courses.

Janner on Presentation

Greville Janner
ISBN 0-09-167421-2
                    Hutchinson Business
A comprehensive guide to presentational skills, ranging from after-dinner speaking to conducting an interview and coping with the media. Excellent reading.

Painless Public Speaking

Sharon Bower
ISBN 0-7225-0765-8   Thorsons
Many books have been written about speaking in public, but this one has a clear, concise style and includes self-teaching worksheets and plenty of practical advice.

Weather at Sea

David Houghton
ISBN 0-906754-23-2   Fernhurst Books
One of the clearest explanations of all the basic principles of meteorology. Written by the met. advisor to many large boating events, the book is also recommended for RYA/DTp Yachtmaster courses.

RYA Publications

The RYA publishes a wide range of compact booklets and handbooks covering every aspect of boating. Those which are particularly relevant as background knowledge to the Powerboat Instructor include:

G2 - International Regulations for Preventing Collisions at Sea

G16 -Safety Boat Handbook

G22 -VHF Radio Telephony

Day Skipper Shorebased Course Notes

Packed with illustrations to demonstrate improved teaching techniques in sail and motor cruising.

Day Skipper Past Papers

Exercises and answers from past shorebased courses.